THE IMPACT OF ANSWERING

"WHAT ARE YOU LOOKING AT?"

AND HOW IT CHANGES EVERYTHING

By Adam J. San Juan

Second edition 2024

For Aaron and Syd, and their children's children's children.

Scout Finch

"People generally see what they look for, and hear what they listen for, and they have a right to subject their children to it, but I can't say I approve or like it."

Contents

Foreword

Connection.

A simple word with a complicated meaning. While the concept is pretty straightforward, humans often misunderstand even a simple word.

I have been a financial planner for almost 30 years, helping families and small business owners plan for their retirement. From the outside, this profession is full of numbers, projections, and risk/reward calculations. But from the inside, this profession is all about connection--connecting with people who seek guidance in their lives, then establishing a high level of trust in a short amount of time.

This can often be difficult for people to do "on demand," which is why the sales industry can sometimes feel disingenuous. For me, it has become second nature due to a strong understanding of people that has taken me decades to master. And not just one type of person, but many people, all of whom have their own personalities!

The skill I have mastered to make meaningful and genuine connections quickly is what I am proud to now introduce to you in this book. It is the art of knowing what you are looking at.

Adam and I met at a networking event in Detroit, Michigan, where we work in the small business retirement plan community. With both of us being in sales, we had a mutual introduction, which I assumed would be quickly followed by the traditional peacocking of accolades that is normal in our industry. I was completely wrong. My first conversation with Adam was like watching a professional athlete excel in their sport. Similar to watching a pro golfer's swing, it is smooth and easy yet powerful. That is how it feels to talk to Adam.

This book can be your first step in becoming more intentional about building connections with people, beginning with your communication skills: how to adapt when people may not communicate like you, thus giving (and receiving) the intended message with precision and avoiding unintended misunderstandings.

If you are in the sales industry and are looking for ways to be more genuine in your approach, this book is for you. If you are in corporate leadership and looking to build more authentic connections with your teams, this book is for you. If you are struggling in personal relationships and looking to understand other humans better, this book is for you.

If you are looking in the mirror and wondering what you are looking at, this book is for you.

Kimberly Enders CFP® CWS® CPFA®

Detroit, Michigan

On Purpose

Why This Book Was Written

My life has made substantial progress since 2020. My two children are surrounded by exceptional people, and their excellent decisions have led to thriving lives. The blessings continue now that they are both married. My daughter gave me two beautiful grandchildren. When my first grandchild learned to walk, her father marveled at her "gaining speed." Ongoing blessings summed up in two words: "gaining speed."

Also, since 2020, I've attended approximately five funerals. I'm not sure if that number is small or large, but life's ebbs and flows prove it's significant. As someone who overthinks, I examined the aftermath of a loss.

The initial shock gives way to a combination of intense grief, sadness, anger, and guilt. Commemorative services provide solace. People often avoid reminders to deal with the numbing sensation. Around 6 to 12 months, reality sets in. The first anniversary of someone's passing is important. Grief can blend with family changes as time passes. The pain reduces after three years, but special occasions can still bring sadness. It dulls and becomes a part of life's pattern. The emptiness remains but is now controllable. Anniversaries carry a lot of emotion and can bring up a wide range of feelings.

In short, after someone passes away, their memory endures, but over time, it fades, and fades and fades, until ultimately...

My biggest fear isn't about money or living a long life. My dread is fading into oblivion. But then the question emerges: "What do you want to be remembered for, Adam?"

I don't want my legacy to be tied to the money I leave behind. That's not appealing to me. As a military brat growing up in modest quarters, money was a foreign concept. I had no rapport with it. As I matured, I never found myself drawn to the pursuit of it. I attribute any wealth I have to a higher power. I've been "well looked after." If you ask me how I'm doing, that's the response you'll get.

Ideas. That's what I want to leave behind: a legacy of ideas. My goal was to raise exceptional children who would go on to have remarkable children themselves, and so on. I hope my granddaughter says to her granddaughter, "Your mom is amazing. I was very blessed to pass down skills to her that I got from my mom. And she got those from her father, your great-great-grandfather, Adam. It traces back to him."

Whether this book sells one copy or a million copies is unimportant. What matters is that a copy gets into the hands of my children as soon as possible.

Why This Topic Was Chosen

In the early days of my marriage, both my wife and I juggled our careers. While I supervised an office, she worked as an RN at the local VA hospital. We had to share a car because of money issues, which meant we had to plan our work schedules carefully.

My job followed a 9-to-5 routine, while her nursing shifts included a.m., p.m., or midnight options. To make it work, she chose p.m. shifts, and I would pick her up around midnight during the week. This pattern led to an intriguing observation.

At 11:30 p.m., I saw a line of cars with Filipino men waiting for their wives outside the hospital entrance. Each time a nurse emerged, the corresponding husband stepped out, opened the door, and waited for her. Once she took her seat inside the car, he would close the door and return to the driver's seat—all without exchanging a word or making eye contact. When three or four wives exited the hospital, the sameness was striking. They all followed the same routine. They all did it the same.

I remember waiting and watching, thinking to myself, "Look at these idiots." But this sight triggered an epiphany: I abhorred uniformity. I despised sameness. I didn't want to blend in with the Filipino husbands. Anonymity bothered me; I yearned for a distinct identity.

The line of Filipino men outside the hospital did something else. It fueled my quest for individuality. I became curious about self-discovery. And along the way, I realized I might be the problem. I had to examine myself before passing judgment. Consider the following phrase: "Lady, you're the fourth person to hit me today." Maybe I was the idiot.

Whether we aim to be alike or different depends on valuing others and knowing ourselves. Knowing yourself and embracing different perspectives reduces criticism and prejudice and improves self-acceptance. Understanding those we may not initially favor helps us coexist more harmoniously.

Reflecting on the past, even before the line of Filipino men, I noticed patterns in my desire to stand out and resist conformity. For instance, sandwiched between two brothers, I avoided their Filipino circles. Even before my wife, Pinays weren't common among my girlfriends. As a mobile DJ in Chicago, I stopped being one because of the abundance of Filipino mobile DJs. My first college semester as an art major shifted to English because I was in a classroom full of Filipino art majors. Apparently, this has been going on for a while.

I need to say my stance is against uniformity, not Filipinos. I'm anti-sameness and anti-default. Countering sameness requires understanding.

I follow three principles in life. The first is knowing what I see.

With time, I've come close to mastering this craft. Like Bruce Lee said, "I fear not the man who has practiced 10,000 kicks once, but I fear the man who has practiced one kick 10,000 times."

This is a kick I've practiced 10,000 times. Should you fear me? No, I'm harmless. I'm just always practicing, trying to figure out what I'm looking at.

And it'd be a shame if I didn't share what I've learned. Not only share it but do it simply and without complexity.

Semi-Spoiler Alert

I learned about the Shapes program for the first time in 2011, during a sales conference in New York. Roughly 150 colleagues from different parts of the country were present in the room. Connie Podesta, renowned for her innovative methodologies, was set to present just before the lunch break.

Connie delivered a strategic and engaging introduction to the Shapes program. She presented two options to the participants: document their perceived Shape on paper or mentally store it. She unpacked systematically each Shape, with its relevance in sales scenarios explained. Emphasizing the traits, behaviors, and communication methods that suit each Shape was her focus. And the approach I took to my professional career changed forever.

Sales conferences prioritize sales techniques and market trends over personal development and interpersonal skills. Studies show that knowledge tends to fade if not utilized within 72 hours. More than a decade later, the Shapes program is still a crucial part of my daily interactions.

I introduced the program to my family during pizza night, seeing if it had potential beyond just business. It was a simple exercise: each drew their Shape on a napkin. My predictions—my wife as a Square, son as a Circle, and daughter as a Wavy Line—were spot-on. This wasn't just a family activity; it was a testament to the program's intuitive design and universal applicability.

The Shapes discussion had a significant influence on my daughter. She wrote a well-received essay for her high school English class on the topic. The discussion it sparked among students and staff was evidence of the model's versatility. I should point out that my daughter received no formal training on my part after our initial conversation at dinner. Her initiative emphasized the program's natural accessibility and ease of transmission.

In all settings where effective communication is crucial, the Shapes program stands out. It can improve team synergy and create genuine connections in any environment because of its simple yet insightful approach.

What is This Book Trying to Solve, and for Whom

This book is a helpful guide for handling situations where good communication and understanding lead to success.

Think about a couple whose strong relationship weakened because of misunderstandings. Picture a first date that didn't go to a second because they misread each other's body language. Imagine a salesperson working hard but struggling to reach sales goals. Unclear comprehension was the problem in each case—emotions, new relationships, or client needs.

The book also talks about leaders, like team leaders or bosses, who struggle to understand their teams and get terrible results. Too much control can halt creativity and new ideas. In coaching, a one-size-fits-all approach hurts unique players, making the team perform worse. Leaders need to understand and accept people's differences, which affect teamwork and success.

To mend relationships, make connections, and succeed as a leader, this book is useful. It explores patterns in thoughts and actions, solving communication problems, and creating connections. It provides tools to understand feelings, learn about personalities, and fit into the world better.

If you've struggled to achieve success and suspect you might be part of the issue, this book is for you. It suits those wanting to understand how relationships work. If you don't value people's thoughts and emotions and prefer basic connections, this book may not suit you. If you think misunderstanding is normal, this book might not match your view.

If you always do things the same way in relationships, you might not grasp why distinct personalities matter. If understanding others isn't an enormous challenge for you, you might not see the tools as very helpful. And if you usually blame others when communication goes wrong, this book might not be the best guide.

If you're content with your communication style and are not very interested in connecting with others, this book might not be the right fit for you.

Building Foundations

PART 1: The Intriguing Intruder: The "Unsettling Presence" Shape

Planet Fitness was my sanctuary. A place where I'd zone out, focusing only on the rhythm of my own breath and the strain of my muscles. However, that tranquility was disrupted when *he* made his appearance. It wasn't just that he was there—it was the flair with which he carried himself. He was more like an evangelist than a regular gym-goer, enthusiastically sharing his workout secrets with anyone who would listen.

His shape was immediately striking. Standing at a mere 5'1", he had this uniquely proportioned body: he was more torso than he was legs, but his legs were stout, suggesting a narrative of many deadlifts and squats.

But it was his attire that truly captured my attention. He donned a beanie, oddly paired with headphones that rested on it like a ceremonial crown. Then there were the leggings beneath his shorts, a snug compression shirt layered under a DIY sleeveless hoodie, wristbands—and let's not forget the weightlifter's belt. And the centerpiece? An unapologetically lush beard.

If Peter Dinklage and Dick's Sporting Goods had a love child, he would be it.

Candidly, my initial reaction was less of intrigue and more of quiet resentment. I knew I was in a judgment-free zone, but I didn't like him.

Audience Insights

This book will start by emphasizing the importance of understanding your audience. We'll talk about why knowing your audience matters, the risks of not knowing them, and how personality models can help you understand them better. We'll explore the choices that have developed over time, leading you from the past to the present. Our focus will be on the significance of truly connecting with your audience and how to leverage this understanding.

The Importance of Knowing Your Audience

Understanding your audience deeply helps you shape your message for them. Learn who they are, what matters to them, and how they speak. This ensures your communication resonates with them. Use relatable examples and language they can connect with. Adjust your tone and style to their preferences. When your message aligns with your audience, it becomes more captivating.

Researching your audience builds trust and credibility. It shows you value them by understanding their viewpoints. Include details that reflect shared beliefs and values. Address their concerns to establish rapport swiftly. This shows that you comprehend their perspective.

Insight into your audience also guides your strategy. Before persuading them, understand their motivations. Adapting to your audience helps you position yourself, highlight important messages, and decide where to reach them. This insight also creates a feedback loop for adjustments based on their responses.

Assumptions about audiences often miss the mark. Conducting thorough research replaces guesswork with facts. This effort pays off through effective communication. When you craft messages tailored to your audience, the connection and resonance are stronger. But what if your assumptions are wrong?

The Consequences of Getting It Wrong

Not understanding your audience can have a negative impact on your messaging in several important ways. If you don't align with what the audience cares about, your communication won't resonate with them. Messages that don't connect to their specific concerns won't engage or motivate them. To be persuasive, you need to understand who you're talking to.

If the audience can't relate to your message, they'll lose interest before you even get to your main point. Furthermore, if you don't articulate your arguments clearly, they might misconstrue your message. Well-meaning communication that's out of touch can even backfire and make them upset. Paying attention to details helps avoid these problems.

Finally, not knowing your audience means you'll waste time and miss opportunities by targeting the wrong people. If you assume things that aren't true, your strategies will fail. This damages your reputation over time as you keep getting things wrong. To fix this, you need to research your audience and make sure you're targeting and messaging correctly.

Dylan vs Dilly Dilly

The Bud Light Dylan Mulvaney campaign of 2022 serves as a sobering reminder of the importance of audience insight in marketing. At its core, the intent behind the campaign was innovative, perhaps even daring. However, where it misstepped was in aligning the messaging with the right audience.

To begin with, one must understand the essence of the Bud Light brand. Historically, Bud Light has positioned itself as the beer for the everyday person—unpretentious, fun, and relatable. Its campaigns create catchphrases that appeal to everyone, like the famous "Dilly Dilly" series in 2017. With Dylan Mulvaney, the intent seemed to deviate from this tried-and-true formula. Instead of focusing on broad appeal, the campaign delved into a niche narrative that didn't resonate with its core audience.

The Mulvaney campaign, while creative, seemed to skip the crucial step of audience testing. Knowing your audience isn't just about demographics or purchasing patterns; it's about understanding their values, aspirations, and cultural touchpoints. Bud Light's primary consumer base may not have related to the essence or humor intended in the Mulvaney campaign, leading to a disconnection.

It's also worth noting that in today's digital age, audiences want authenticity. Customers want genuine relationships with brands. If marketing feels fake or out of touch, they'll ignore it and may complain on social media. The Mulvaney campaign, in missing its mark, inadvertently created a chasm between the brand and its loyalists.

The Dylan Mulvaney campaign's failure shows how important it is to understand your audience. No matter how innovative or groundbreaking a marketing idea may seem, it must, at its heart, speak to the brand's core audience. When brands stray too far from this central tenet, they risk not only the success of a single campaign but also the trust and loyalty they've built over the years.

The Bud Light marketing example shows how important it is to match your message with your audience on a larger scale. Let's examine how this applies to smaller, more personal interactions. Large or small, the same still applies. Understanding your audience is key.

To communicate, you must understand the person you're talking to. There are many ways to do this, like using formal programs, having structured conversations, or just straight observation. Believability, usefulness, and practicality are important, no matter the method. All of this helps you answer the question, "What are you looking at?"

Using Personality Identification Models to Get It Right

Personality Identification Models (PIMs) are useful tools for understanding how people think. They sort out common traits, values, behaviors, and ways of processing information. This helps create detailed descriptions of different people. By connecting real observations to these personality types, we can see a more comprehensive picture of different groups. PIMs enhance audience understanding.

PIMs also show what motivates each type, like the desire for success, social connection, or independence. This helps create messages that speak to these desires. The models also suggest what kind of tone, style, and language to use. Figuring out where people are on the scale of being introverted, emotional, or open lets you adjust how you talk to them.

PIMs help split audiences by personality instead of just basic details. Grouping by behavior is better than age or gender. These models make it easy to talk about different audience needs. They prevent misunderstandings that may arise from messages not matching personalities.

Personality Identification Models: Past to Present

Next, we'll explore how PIMs can reveal motivations, communication styles, and habits. This helps us connect effectively with people. We'll start by checking out the earliest models, like ancient Greece's Four Temperaments theory. Then we'll talk about popular ones used today, such as MBTI, the Big Five, and DISC.

To understand these models, we'll see how well they work in real life and if they're easy to use. We will make a comparison to identify strengths and weaknesses. Finally, we'll discuss models that find a balance between various factors for optimal results.

The Earliest Personality Identification Models Known

In 400 BC, Hippocrates created the Four Temperaments Theory to understand personalities. He tried to group human behaviors and traits into categories. He thought that four bodily fluids—blood, phlegm, yellow bile, and black bile—affected how people acted, felt, and thought.

Hippocrates connected these fluids to four personality types: sanguine, phlegmatic, choleric, and melancholic. Sanguines were friendly because of their warm blood. Phlegmatics were calm because of the cool phlegm. Cholerics were ambitious and leaders because of their fiery yellow bile. Melancholics were thoughtful and anxious because of black bile. Everyone had a mix of these traits.

Even though this idea isn't as advanced as modern psychology, Hippocrates was one of the first to suggest sorting personality traits. He realized the need to explain why people behave and think in certain ways. His theory influenced later ideas that looked at how a person's surroundings and thoughts shape their personality.

The Most Popular Personality Identification Models Used Today

The Myers-Briggs Type Indicator (MBTI) is a well-known model used to identify personalities. There are 16 types based on 4 preferences: extroversion/introversion, sensing/intuition, thinking/feeling, and judging/perceiving. The MBTI helps define distinct personality traits while valuing all preferences. It's used in careers, teamwork, leadership training, and more.

Another proven model is the Big Five or Five-Factor Model. It examines five dominant traits: openness, conscientiousness, extroversion, agreeableness, and neuroticism. It's detailed and backed by data. But it doesn't focus on growth like the MBTI.

DISC is simpler and useful for social interactions. It sorts personalities into Dominant, Influential, Steady, or Conscientious types. It shows different communication styles and behaviors. DISC is beneficial for professional training, such as conflict resolution or teamwork.

Each of these models is well-established and provides different perspectives. They help us understand ourselves and work better with distinct personalities. It's beneficial to have knowledge about all of them.

Measuring the Efficacy of Personality Identification Models

The three major criteria for judging personality frameworks are validity, usefulness, and usability.

Verifying the accuracy of a framework is essential to prove its effectiveness. Without solid evidence and precision, the framework isn't trustworthy.

Usefulness means the framework should offer practical advice that we can use. It can improve our communication, relationships, and self-awareness. If a framework only gives us ideas without real-world value, it's not very helpful.

Last, it should be easy to use. Complexity and time consumption discourage framework usage. We need simple and user-friendly assessments to get people interested. Complicated ones might be accurate, but they won't be useful if people don't use them.

In short, a personality framework needs to be valid, useful, and easy to use to be truly helpful.

Measuring the Efficacy of the Most Popular Personality Identification Models

The Big Five model does well in all three areas we care about. Many tests over the years have confirmed its accuracy. The five fundamental traits it looks at are also helpful in real-life situations, like talking to people, leading teams, and working together. Although more complex than DISC, you can grasp it with some learning.

The Myers-Briggs model is well-researched and has gained significant popularity. Though people may have heard of the distinct personality types it talks about, they might not always be aware of how to apply them in a practical way like they do with DISC. Although many people are aware of it, you need further training to comprehend it properly.

DISC lacks sufficient scientific research. However, it's useful for practical purposes. It gives you quick advice on how to change your behavior. It's the easiest one to understand, even if you have learned little about it. The lack of strong research behind it means we should proceed with caution.

I don't use any of these models.

Navigating Personalities and Relationships through Shapes

PART 2: The Gym's Whisperer: The "Persistent Elf" Shape

As time moved forward, it became apparent that avoiding him was an exercise in futility. He had this almost magnetic presence, always in the periphery of my workout sessions. And then, the inevitable happened. Mid-squat, I heard that distinct voice— tinged with an enthusiasm that was hard to place, a mix of Mickey Mouse and a sprinkle of Latin rhythm. "You'll get a deeper engagement in your glutes if you put a weight plate under your heels," he chimed, sharing his unsolicited wisdom.

Before I could even process or respond, he was gone, darting to another corner, no doubt to share another pearl of wisdom. It was like witnessing a gym spirit, offering guidance, and then disappearing before one could even thank him.

Shapes Personality Identification Model: Traits, Temperaments, and Effectiveness

In the upcoming sections, we'll inspect the Shapes PIM. This includes its four dominant personality types. We'll discuss important parts of Shapes and how they relate to the Four Temperaments Theory. While Shapes is more current, it shares some similarities with the ancient theory. We'll also see how effective Shapes is using the criteria we reviewed earlier. Shapes is a strong choice for improving everyday interactions with its mix of lasting wisdom and practical usefulness.

But first, an Indian parable about five blind men and the elephant:

There were five blind men who had heard about a mysterious creature called an elephant but had no idea what it looked like. Each blind man touched a different part of the elephant and came away with a very different impression of what an elephant must be like.

The first blind man felt the elephant's sturdy side and declared, "An elephant is like a wall!" The second blind man touched the tusk and said, "An elephant is like a spear!" The third blind man felt the squirming trunk and decided, "An elephant is like a snake!" The fourth blind man touched the knee and concluded, "An elephant is like a tree!" The fifth blind man felt the ear flap and insisted, "An elephant is like a fan!"

Each blind man was convinced that their experience of just one part equated to understanding the whole elephant. Of course, they were all mistaken. Though the elephant had qualities in common with a wall, spear, snake, tree, and fan, it was far more complex than any of those individual impressions.

The Key Aspects of the Shapes Personality Identification Model

The Shapes program breaks people into four dominant personality types: Circle, Square, Triangle, and Wavy

Line. Shapes help us understand ourselves, communicate better, and have better relationships.

Think of the parable of the blind men and the elephant. The men's perceptions of the elephant varied because of their limited knowledge. When we deal with people, we might only see one side of their personality. The Shapes model helps us see the entire picture.

Circles are warm and caring, focusing on relationships. Squares think logically, like structure and details, and do things efficiently. Triangles are leaders who like deciding and getting results. Wavy Lines are creative, like change, and are open to new ideas.

Knowing these four types helps us understand how people fit together or where they might have problems. By knowing these Shapes, we can use our strengths and know our weaknesses. If the blind men discussed the elephant, they would learn more. Using Shapes helps us communicate and adapt to distinct personalities.

The Connection Between Shapes and the Four Temperaments

Hippocrates' theory of four temperaments and the modern four Shapes personality types are connected. Despite being developed at different times, both theories categorize personality traits.

The warm and caring Circle is like the outgoing and friendly sanguine. They share a love for socializing and connecting with people.

The thoughtful, organized melancholic matches the structured, detail-oriented Square. They both have a concern for achieving exactness.

The strong-willed choleric temperament is a lot like the goal-focused, confident Triangle. Both are leaders and take charge.

The easygoing and adaptable phlegmatic is a good match for the flexible and creative Wavy Line who dislikes conflict.

Four temperaments come from body fluids, while Shapes come from psychology theories. Each Shape type has a greater assortment of variations. People might have a mix of traits instead of just one category. Despite the similarities, Shapes aims to enhance Hippocrates' theory.

Measuring the Efficacy of Shapes

The Shapes PIM's reliability is uncertain due to a lack of scientific evidence and statistics for its four types. Unlike Myers-Briggs and the Big Five, Shapes is based on observation and grouping rather than scientific testing. As a result, we're left wondering if it's accurate or opinion-based. While the Shapes PIM is useful, it's more speculative than conclusive.

But the Shapes PIM is good for practical use. The four shapes help with self-improvement, job growth, leadership, and relationships. By understanding Circles, Squares, Triangles, and Wavy Lines, you can figure out why you and others act in certain ways. This enables teams to work together more productively, engage in meaningful dialogue, assist each other more efficiently, and gain a greater understanding of one another.

The Shapes PIM is easy to comprehend. Understanding the details doesn't require a deep understanding of psychology. This is about Shapes and their descriptions. It requires minimal training, making it accessible to many. The simple language and ideas let you quickly see your Shape or guess someone else's. Despite a lack of scientific evidence, its simplicity makes it both useful and engaging.

Shape Recognition: Observation

Let's say you're in a group, casually observing the people around you. Someone catches your interest from afar. Remembering that understanding comes first, you switch on your "Shape identification mode" to learn more before you approach and engage with them.

You observe their actions and nonverbal expressions from a distance. What could this person be telling you about their Shape? Could they be a Circle, Square, Triangle, or Wavy Line? As you keep observing in different situations—social, work, personal—do you notice any consistent signs?

Imagine approaching, making eye contact, and shaking hands. What hints do you notice in those first important moments? While you talk, do you focus on how they communicate, choose their words, and use their tone? What questions can you ask to figure out their Shape?

If you're still uncertain of their Shape after speaking with them, pay close attention to the way they end the conversation. What can you learn from a voicemail or a text they send? Somewhere between watching from a distance and pressing phone buttons, you'll find the answer to that big question: What are you looking at?

The upcoming sections will lead you through this process, from recognizing the characteristics of each Shape from afar to the detailed elements that form each individual Shape. As you observe and communicate with others, you'll get better at identifying each one.

So, what are you looking at? The answer may be right in front of you.

Recognizing Shapes by Behavioral Patterns and Body Language

Circle: Key Behavioral Patterns

Circles have a talent for spreading positivity and being social, as their name implies. They are very sociable and can make new friends, energize conversations, and share their enthusiasm. They often travel around groups, bringing energy to social events. Due to their outgoing nature, they're great at networking and forming relationships.

Their concern for others is crucial. Circles are fantastic listeners who can understand others' feelings. They're compassionate when people share their joys and struggles, showing genuine empathy. When they listen, they're patient and focused, radiating a secure presence that invites trust. For advice and support, many seek Circles.

Peacemaking is a common role for Circles in teams and relationships. They're adept at understanding the feelings and perspectives of others, and can often find a way to address and resolve disagreements in a peaceful manner. This Shape prioritizes teamwork and harmony and strives to reach solutions that satisfy everyone. When tension arises, their presence helps keep everyone composed. People often rely on Circles to keep everyone connected.

Circles are social, empathetic listeners, and skilled at resolving conflicts. They bring people together, make others feel understood, and create harmony in groups. With their positive attitude, they lift the spirits of those around them.

Circle: Key Aspects of Body Language

A Circle's body language radiates warmth and openness, which encourages trust and engagement. Their body language expresses openness and ease, conveying friendliness and approachability. When they listen, they maintain eye contact and nod to show they're paying attention. Circles also reflect others' emotions through their facial expressions. Smiling is their way of expressing joy, and they show empathy by furrowing their brows when someone is sad.

Circles are skilled at using nonverbal cues to make everyone feel included. They use inviting, broad gestures to coax timid individuals into conversations. Circles also use welcoming actions like open arms, leaning in while talking, and offering reassuring pats on the hand during trying times. Their comforting presence draws people in.

Even when meeting someone for the first time, Circles are friendly. They make eye contact without hesitation and give genuine smiles to show they're open to talking. Their relaxed posture and tilted heads show they're ready to share thoughts and feelings. Circles can move between groups, using warm looks and gestures to join conversations. Nonverbal communication comes naturally to Circles, helping them connect with others.

Circles are good at nonverbal communication that make people feel at ease. They create a space for meaningful conversations by being encouraging, attentive, and inviting. For Circles, body language is a way to express their empathetic nature.

Square: Key Behavioral Patterns

The Square personality type is all about accuracy and being precise. They pay close attention to details and are good at finding even the smallest mistakes. When they work on a project, they make sure everything is just right. Squares are ideal for tasks that require careful attention and can help prevent mistakes.

Squares are also excellent at planning and organizing. They prefer a simple plan and step-by-step execution. This makes them good at managing projects and teams. They bring order to the group and help everyone work together smoothly. They're also good leaders because they help others to be efficient.

Squares prefer stability and routine. They decide based on facts and logic, not emotions. Having a set routine makes them feel comfortable, while unexpected changes can be stressful. Creating structure and order is how Squares make sense of things and bring logic to their surroundings.

Being accurate, organized, and logical are the strengths of Squares. Their behaviors show how they excel at paying attention to details, creating structure, and staying focused on practical goals. Using these strengths helps Squares avoid mistakes and stay productive.

Square: Key Aspects of Body Language

Squares project an image of calm and control through their body language. Even when they're stressed, they maintain a composed posture. You won't see their emotions easily in their facial expressions or gestures. Squares prefer movements that are precise and purposeful, avoiding any extra actions that could make them seem less confident.

When they talk, Squares like to keep it straightforward. They speak in a measured tone and use eye contact and nods to show they're listening. They don't use a lot of gestures while speaking; instead, they use them to emphasize certain points. Despite the excitement or intensity of a conversation, their speech never wavers or changes.

Even though Squares feel emotions like everyone else, they show them less openly. They focus on using factual language rather than emotional words. But if you pay close attention, you might catch subtle signs like tightened lips, raised eyebrows, or tapping fingers that reveal their feelings. It takes some patience to understand Squares' less obvious emotional expressions, but it helps build a deeper connection.

Squares' body language is all about control and discipline. They have a composed presence and communicate efficiently. You can see their feelings through their eyes and subtle expressions, even though their Shape is less expressive. Paying attention to these cues can help you connect better with Squares.

Triangle: Key Behavioral Patterns

Achieving goals is the top priority that motivates Triangles. They set lofty goals and work relentlessly to reach them, even in the face of challenges. The unwavering dedication to achieving personal and professional objectives speaks volumes about their commitment to success. By holding themselves and their teams accountable for results, Triangles inspire ongoing improvement.

Deciding is a natural skill for Triangles, which gives them confidence to take control of situations. They can make sound choices even when things are unclear or tough. This ability to act swiftly and provide guidance earns them leadership positions. They lead teams to accomplish their objectives with assertiveness.

Triangles step up their game when competition arises. They enjoy overcoming challenges and testing their skills. Competition, for them, isn't just about triumphing over others. They use their competitive spirit to motivate personal growth and success. Improving is a response to losses.

Goal-orientation, decisiveness, and competitiveness are traits of Triangles. These qualities help Triangles lead teams and achieve results with their action-oriented approaches. Embracing these tendencies helps them build momentum.

Triangle: Key Aspects of Body Language

Triangles exude confidence through their body language. They stand tall and walk purposefully, showing they're in control. Making direct eye contact tells others they're sure of themselves. Their gestures are strong and deliberate, like firm handshakes, direct hand motions, and emphatic nods. They attract attention with their energetic movements.

Their facial expressions mirror their determination. They show intense happiness when they reach goals and a serious expression when facing challenges. Triangles' body language reflects their competitive spirit and their eagerness for challenges. They rarely show nervous habits or slouch, always looking like leaders.

Even when they're not active, Triangles show their focus. They sit or stand with a straight posture and a concentrated look. Their presence demands respect and attention. If you pay close attention, you might notice subtle signs like tapping fingers or pressed lips, showing their eagerness to get things done. Triangles value their bold body language. Being around them feels inspiring.

Triangles work on body language that's strong but also inviting. They display their confidence and determination in how they stand and move. Their actions show they're ready to tackle challenges. Triangles know the power of nonverbal communication in displaying leadership qualities. Just being around them can make you want to act.

Wavy Line: Key Behavioral Patterns

The Wavy Line personality is all about creativity and imagination. They come up with new solutions that don't follow the usual rules. They question things and think up ideas that others might miss. Their creativity helps them solve problems in clever ways.

Being adaptable is another strong trait of Wavy Lines. They're not bothered by change; in fact, they're inspired by it. When things shift, Wavy Lines can adjust and handle new situations. They stay calm and grounded, even when things are uncertain. Teams can rely on Wavy Lines to help them stay strong in tough times.

Empathy and kindness are common traits of Wavy Lines. They can understand what others need without even saying it. People love talking to them because they listen without judging. They give support and wise advice to individuals and groups. Their caring nature helps build strong relationships.

Wavy Lines' unique approach, flexibility, and emotional awareness make them a valuable asset. They bring fresh ideas while also helping to keep things organized. They make connections between people and help them understand each other. Their ability to adapt helps everyone grow.

Wavy Line: Key Aspects of Body Language

The way Wavy Lines move and express themselves reflects their creative nature. They use their hands to emphasize their words, and their faces show their emotions, from curiosity to excitement. Their posture is relaxed yet interested, leaning in when they're engaged. Even when they're not moving, you can sense their energy, ready to burst out in enthusiastic gestures.

Wavy Lines make eye contact and nod to show they're paying attention. They adjust their tone of voice to match the feelings in a conversation. When you're around them, you feel like they're listening and interested in what you're saying.

Their artistic side comes out in their clothes and style. They don't worry too much about fitting in, and they express themselves freely. Sometimes they might touch your arm showing they understand. Their friendly and enthusiastic nonverbal cues let you know they're open to connecting on a genuine level.

Wavy Lines use their body language to express their creativity and emotions. Their movements and engagement show that they're eager to understand and connect with others. Through their warm and adaptable nonverbal communication, you can see their empathy and imagination shine.

Recognizing Shapes in Social Settings

Social events offer excellent opportunities to see how Shapes' unique traits play out. As people mix and connect, their natural personality traits become clear in how they act. By noticing certain cues, we can spot Circles, Squares, Triangles, and Wavy Lines from across the room. They show their social tendencies through how they talk, interact, and the roles they take on. Whether they're quiet or outgoing, each Shape has its own marks. Learning these cues helps us quickly identify Shapes in a social setting, giving us insights before we even talk to them. Let's explore how Shapes reveal their traits in these situations when they're just being themselves.

Circles in Social Settings

People with Circle personalities enjoy social gatherings where they can exude a friendly and open attitude. They actively listen and understand, making people feel important. If someone is going through a tough time, Circles provide comfort through kind words or a reassuring touch. They steer conversations away from disagreements to keep things peaceful.

Circles want everyone to feel welcome, so they're great at introducing people and forming connections. They smoothly move between different groups, connecting them together. They encourage storytelling and fun moments that create bonds. No one feels left out when Circles are around.

Their primary goal is to create a sense of belonging. Circles boost their friends' confidence and inspire them. They build a powerful community by being supportive without judgment. While respecting differences, Circles enjoy the common human experience that connects us all. Their warmth, understanding, and listening skills make friendships meaningful.

Look for the person who brings people together and makes them feel accepted. Find the one who understands others emotionally. Notice the person who maintains harmony in groups. When you spot a Circle, you're finding the heart of the group—someone who truly cares.

Squares in Social Settings

Square personalities reveal themselves through their organized and responsible actions in group settings. Their punctuality shows that they respect others' time. When they talk, they stick to the main points and keep the conversation clear. Squares take charge of planning events to make sure everything goes smoothly. They also follow social rules and norms.

Practical solutions are the focus of Squares for problem-solving. They value traditional ideas but are open to respectful debate. They feel most comfortable discussing concrete topics on which they have expertise. Squares freely show their appreciation for others' efforts and accomplishments.

For Squares, family and community are important. In social gatherings, they work well as part of a team, collaborating to achieve common goals. They're the ones who welcome new people and make introductions. As friends, they offer reliable support. Their consistency brings stability during both good times and challenges.

Keep an eye out for someone who's organized and values responsibility. Notice the planner who's focused on tasks and schedules. Identify the logical thinker who's good at finding solutions. When you come across a Square, you're seeing someone who brings order and dedication, even when things get busy.

Triangles in Social Settings

Triangle personalities are the ones who stand out as leaders in groups. They have a strong and confident presence that often leads them to take charge, whether it's in conversations or planning activities. Triangles share their goals, achievements, and welcome challenges that help them grow.

Triangles are assertive in how they communicate. They share their opinions directly but also listen carefully to others. When they're planning events, they set clear goals and figure out the best ways to achieve them. Triangles love to do well in situations where there's competition or obstacles to overcome.

Triangles want to motivate and inspire their friends while also having some fun. They're skilled at balancing serious conversations with spur-of-the-moment fun. Triangles are quick to seize opportunities to connect with others or create networks. They're tough, adaptable, and always focused on getting results in social situations.

Keep an eye out for the person who takes charge and leads the way. Notice the planner who sets clear goals. Recognize the confident presence that gets people excited. When you see a Triangle, you're looking at someone who encourages others to do their best by being confident, having big ideas, and working hard. They bring out the best in the people around them.

Wavy Lines in Social Settings

Wavy Line personalities truly shine in group settings as engaged participants. They easily move between different people, using their humor and stories to bring shy individuals into conversations. The Wavy Line expresses their excitement through lively gestures and facial expressions. They're quick to understand and offer emotional support when someone needs it.

In conversations, the Wavy Line can smoothly switch topics to find common ground with others. They don't stick to strict plans; instead, they prefer going with the flow and being spontaneous. The Wavy Line works to keep everyone getting along, stepping in to help if there are disagreements. Their creativity comes out in unique ideas and activities.

The Wavy Line wants to have new experiences and connect with others on an authentic level. They create an atmosphere where people can be themselves and share their feelings openly. The Wavy Line is kind and caring, making sure everyone feels welcome and accepted. They bring energy to social gatherings, and their empathetic nature helps to keep people grounded.

Keep an eye out for the person who tells engaging stories and makes everyone feel involved. Notice the flexible networker who brings different people together. Pay attention to the supportive friend who encourages open conversations and harmony. If you spot someone like this, you've found a Wavy Line. They bring people together through their openness, creativity, and empathy, making everyone's experience better.

Recognizing Shapes in Professional Settings

Learn about Shapes' personalities by watching how they work. Even in a formal work environment, one can still observe patterns in how people lead, communicate, and approach tasks based on their Shape. Paying attention to specific cues can help you identify Circles, Squares, Triangles, and Wavy Lines from across the meeting room. Their innate tendencies manifest in their work style, interactions with colleagues, and project roles. Knowing professional cues can help you identify personalities before collaborating. In the workplace, professionals display understated yet noticeable Shape traits that are highly valued.

Circles in Professional Settings

At work, people recognize Circles for their friendly and relationship-focused traits. Their empathy and conflict resolution skills make them valuable team members who excel in collaboration. The focus of Circles is to promote unity by finding solutions that address the group's needs.

Diplomacy is involved in their communication style, offering feedback that aims to help instead of criticize. Circles promote emotional openness and encourage others to do the same. They excel at building professional connections within and beyond their organization.

Circles adopt a supportive approach that fosters the development of others when in leadership positions. The environment they create values individual growth and a balanced work-life. They avoid confrontations, but they solve issues by finding mutual agreement. They show a balance of empathy and stability.

Top Five Jobs for Circles

Counselor or Therapist: Circles' empathetic and active listening skills make them great counselors or therapists who can create a safe space for individuals to share their thoughts and emotions.

Social Worker: Circles' caring nature and ability to connect with others suit social work, where they can advocate for vulnerable populations and provide support to those in need.

Teacher or Educator: Circles can excel in teaching roles by creating nurturing classroom environments, helping students feel valued, and fostering positive learning atmospheres.

Nurse or Healthcare Professional: With their compassion and emotional intelligence, Circles can shine in nursing roles, providing reassurance and comfort to patients' well-being.

Customer Service Representative: Circles' friendly and empathetic demeanor makes them well-suited for customer service roles, offering excellent support and addressing clients' concerns.

Worst Five Jobs for Circles

Sales Representative: The pressure and competitiveness of sales roles may not align with Circles' preference for harmony and non-confrontational communication.

Competitive Business Executive: Roles requiring intense competition and assertiveness might not be the best fit for Circles, who prioritize collaboration and empathy.

Solo Researcher: Positions that involve isolated and independent research with little interaction may not fulfill Circles' need for social engagement.

Mechanical or Technical Positions: Technical roles that lack human interaction might not leverage Circles' strengths in empathy and relationship-building.

Isolated Data Analyst: Jobs focused on data analysis with little interaction may not provide Circles with the social engagement and collaborative opportunities they thrive on.

Squares in Professional Settings

The workplace tends to take note of individuals who have an organized and careful approach, which is often associated with Squares. These individuals can best exercise their analytical and organizational skills in a structured environment. Squares establish definite objectives and pursue them with methodical precision. They place great importance on dependability and timely fulfillment of deadlines.

Squares have a straightforward communication style, presenting clear and concise points. Before beginning tasks in full, they comprehend the regulations, methods, and anticipations. Squares rely on data analysis and calculated risk-taking for decision-making. Predictability is preferred and established procedures are comforting to them.

Collaboration helps Squares achieve efficiency. Group projects become more organized with their involvement. Squares respect authority but also share their opinions. They take pride in delivering quality work that meets goals and deadlines. To recognize Squares is to see their hard work, practical thinking, and pursuit of excellence.

Top Five Jobs for Squares

Accountant: Squares' attention to detail and meticulous nature suit accounting roles that require precision and accuracy in financial management.

Project Manager: Squares' organizational skills and structured thinking make them effective project managers who can coordinate tasks and timelines.

Data Analyst: Squares' analytical mindset and methodical approach are assets in roles that involve analyzing and interpreting data to make informed decisions.

Quality Control Specialist: With their focus on accuracy, Squares can excel in roles that involve inspecting products or processes to ensure they meet quality standards.

Research Scientist: Squares' dedication to thorough research and logical problem-solving makes them well-suited for scientific roles that require systematic investigation.

Worst Five Jobs for Squares

Creative Artist: Roles demanding unconventional thinking and artistic expression might not align with Squares' preference for structure and rules.

Event Planner: The dynamic and often unpredictable nature of event planning might challenge Square's need for predictability and routine.

Performer or Actor: Jobs that involve spontaneous creativity and improvisation may not utilize Squares' preference for methodical preparation.

Adventure Tour Guide: The unpredictability of outdoor activities and varying group dynamics might not align with Squares' need for stability and order.

Crisis Management Specialist: Roles requiring quick, unstructured decision-making in high-pressure situations might not align with Squares' preference for careful planning and analysis.

Triangles in Professional Settings

Achieving goals and taking charge are the strong suits of Triangles in the workplace. Defining objectives and working towards them is key to their success. Triangles are effective leaders who make quick decisions and provide clear direction to teams. They value logic and data over emotions when making decisions and prioritize efficiency in executing plans.

They communicate assertively and directly with the goal of achieving tangible outcomes. Their preference is for clear directions and feedback that enhances performance. Triangles work well in teams, but they also enjoy working independently and appreciate control over their work. They possess planning expertise, ensuring teams stay on track to achieve their objectives.

Competitiveness and facing challenges are how Triangles demonstrate their expertise. They prevent avoidable disagreements that may impede group advancement. Understanding a Triangle's focus on results, strong leadership, and drive to succeed is key to identifying them.

Top Five Jobs for Triangles

CEO or Business Leader: Triangles' decisive and goal-oriented nature suits leadership roles where they can drive organizations towards success.

Project Manager: Triangles' strategic thinking and ability to make quick decisions make them effective in managing complex projects.

Sales Manager: Their competitive drive and assertive communication style make Triangles effective in leading sales teams and achieving targets.

Marketing Director: Triangles' goal-focused mindset and strategic thinking can benefit them in creating and executing marketing campaigns.

Lawyer or Legal Professional: Triangles' analytical thinking and assertiveness can be assets in legal roles that involve negotiation and problem-solving.

Worst Five Jobs for Triangles

Counselor or Therapist: Roles that require extensive empathy and emotional support may not align with Triangles' assertive and goal-driven approach.

Creative Artist: Jobs demanding unconventional thinking and free expression might not align with Triangles' preference for structured approaches.

Social Worker: Roles involving prolonged emotional engagement and empathy might not suit Triangles' more task-oriented and results-driven nature.

Scientist or Researcher: Positions requiring patience for meticulous experimentation and prolonged analysis might not align with Triangles' preference for action.

Wildlife Biologist: Fieldwork and research that require prolonged observation and patience may not align with Triangles' preference for fast-paced decision-making.

Wavy Lines in Professional Settings

The workplace recognizes Wavy Lines for their creativity and collaboration. They approach problem-solving with innovative thinking and are comfortable with change and unpredictability. Wavy Lines have an emotional impact, diplomatically connecting and persuading.

They excel in brainstorming sessions as team members, bringing forth fresh ideas. They can transition to new tasks and projects because of their adaptability. Wavy Lines value strong professional relationships and motivate their colleagues to succeed.

The contagious optimism and enthusiasm of Wavy Lines affect the work environment. They will take measured risks that result in personal development. Acknowledge their diverse skills in creativity, leadership, and intuition.

Top Five Jobs for Wavy Lines

Creative Director: Wavy Lines' imaginative and innovative nature can thrive in roles where they lead creative teams and develop artistic projects.

Marketing Specialist: Their creative thinking and adaptability can be assets in developing unique marketing strategies and campaigns.

Event Planner: Wavy Lines' love for novelty and social engagement can make them excellent event planners, creating memorable experiences.

Human Resources Coordinator: Their ability to understand and connect with diverse individuals can benefit them in fostering a harmonious workplace.

Counselor or Therapist: Wavy Lines' empathetic nature and creative problem-solving can contribute to creating supportive and nurturing therapy environments.

Worst Five Jobs for Wavy Lines

Financial Analyst: Roles that involve meticulous number crunching and data analysis may not align with Wavy Lines' preference for creative expression.

Auditor: Jobs that require a focus on strict regulations and routine examination of financial records might not suit Wavy Lines' desire for variety.

Quality Control Inspector: Roles involving repetitive and detail-oriented tasks might not align with Wavy Lines' preference for dynamic and creative work.

Actuary: Positions requiring extensive statistical analysis and predictive modeling may not resonate with Wavy Lines' imaginative and non-linear thinking.

Systems Analyst: Jobs focused on structured technical analysis and routine problem-solving may not align with Wavy Lines' preference for innovative approaches.

Recognizing Shapes in Family and Personal Relationships

In family settings, we get a close look at Shapes' fundamental traits through their interactions with loved ones. Their true tendencies in communication, conflict resolution, and nurturing roles come to light when they're not at work. We can identify Shapes by looking for consistent patterns in their families. We can understand behaviors in personal settings by recognizing social cues. It's worth studying how Shapes show trust in close relationships.

Circles in Family and Personal Relationships

Circles exhibit their caring and supportive nature in relationships with family and friends. Their kindness establishes an environment that is both welcoming and trustworthy. They are skilled listeners who provide emotional support during tough times and assist those they care about.

In conflicts, Circles serve as peacemakers and strive to preserve harmony. Instead of direct confrontation, they encourage open conversations to find common ground. They use a collaborative approach to find compromise and understanding. Their expertise lies in managing relationships and restoring harmony.

Circles should be cautious not to place others above themselves. They may overlook self-care because of their emphasis on others. They create strong connections and uplift those around them through their emotional intelligence. By genuinely showing interest, they make people feel safe to share. To spot a Circle is to locate the center of a family—a calming and nurturing presence that assists and directs every member.

Squares in Family and Personal Relationships

The organized approach of Squares brings structure, stability, and clear thinking to family dynamics. Routines and traditions provide comfort and significance. Dependable planners, Squares ensure smooth operations. They effectively handle resources and keep their home environment clean.

Squares communicate directly and concisely. Before deciding, they analyze situations carefully. They prioritize their goals as partners and provide dependable support that motivates their loved ones. Their strong focus on tasks and accomplishments may overshadow emotional connections.

Squares use logical reasoning to find practical solutions during conflicts. They highly respect family hierarchies and authority roles. Squares need to be careful not to burden others with too much pressure, despite their high standards. Consistency and reliability bring comfort and strengthen relationships. The Square is the one in the family who provides stability and responsibility with a practical perspective.

Triangles in Family and Personal Relationships

Triangles' ambitious nature makes them natural leaders in their families. They make simple plans to achieve lofty goals. A Triangle is self-assured in problem-solving and leading their loved ones to flourish. Their strong focus on results may affect emotional connections.

Efficient decision-making is a priority for Triangles, and they assert their opinions. They encourage their loved ones to be independent and self-directed. They inspire their family members to believe in themselves by their confidence and determination.

Triangles must balance their authority by showing empathy and promoting collaboration. If they aren't careful listeners, their strong leadership can cause conflicts. The overall result of Triangles' determination in setting strategic goals is the success of their families. We can identify a Triangle by recognizing the leader who guides their family towards greater accomplishments.

Wavy Lines in Family and Personal Relationships

Wavy Lines can improve family dynamics by bringing warmth, understanding, and enjoyment. Their outgoing nature fosters family members to engage in fun activities together. They are compassionate and can listen empathetically to provide emotional support. Wavy Lines encourage their loved ones and motivate them to pursue their interests.

Wavy Lines can easily adapt to changes in family situations because of their flexibility. At home, they prioritize peace and avoid conflicts. Those around them may need to be patient when dealing with their unpredictable spontaneity. In addition, their habit of committing to social events may limit their availability for other engagements.

Wavy Lines create a positive and spontaneous vibe that boosts joy in relationships. Wavy Lines welcome everyone's differences and create a respectful environment. The presence of a Wavy Line in the family is equivalent to finding the origin of laughter, empathy, and shared experiences.

Recognizing Shapes by Their Observed Weaknesses

The strengths of each Shape have been observed. We have evaluated their exceptional traits, affecting their engagement and contributions. Let's now turn our attention to the other side of things. Every strength has an opposite side, which casts a distinct shadow. We could consider their weaknesses as the opposite of their strengths, yet there's still more to discover. Understanding what happens when these strengths go too far is crucial.

Circle Weaknesses

Circles' willingness to help others can lead to them taking on too much. They find it difficult to set boundaries, which can cause exhaustion if they're frequently overburdened. It's crucial to learn how to set boundaries and take care of oneself. To be there for others, Circles must not neglect their own needs.

Circles avoid conflict, yet this approach may leave issues unresolved. It's important to speak up calmly when there's an issue, even if they prefer harmony. The ability to communicate assertively and find solutions can enhance their confidence. Balancing self-esteem and growth opportunities is crucial when dealing with criticism.

Circles may face difficulty in delegating tasks and making choices. Preventing an overwhelming situation is possible by learning to delegate and make timely choices. While the intentions are good, finding a balance is crucial for Circles. They can help others set boundaries, communicate openly, and inspire those around them. These areas will grow based on their natural strengths.

Square Weaknesses

Squares may feel uneasy with change because of their preference for organization and certainty. They stick to familiar ways of thinking and may overlook novel concepts. Squares can grow and gain confidence by embracing calculated risks and adaptability, even if it feels uneasy. It takes time to learn how to be flexible, but it's worth the effort.

It can be a challenge to strive for perfection. The Square personality may be too critical of themselves and others, resulting in excess stress. Perfection may not always be possible, and it's important for them to understand that. Squares can concentrate on gradual improvement, but if they plan too much, they run the risk of missing deadlines.

Squares can grow by learning to accept help from others and sharing their emotions. When teammates use their strengths to contribute, everyone wins. Although expressing emotions can feel uncomfortable, it strengthens connections.

Triangle Weaknesses

Triangles can be overzealous in their pursuit of completing a goal. As a result, they can come off as impatient and selfish. They should combine realistic timelines with a sense of urgency. They should focus their competitive nature inward, rather than trying to outdo others. Focusing on teamwork encourages them to strive for collective success.

Triangles should prioritize emotional intelligence as well. They should not ignore human needs while focusing on results. They can improve their understanding by listening carefully and considering different viewpoints. Although they prefer independence, asking for help when necessary reduces workloads and fosters trust.

If Triangles are excessively confident, they may disregard challenges and different perspectives. Humility and openness to feedback can prevent this. They should avoid making hasty decisions by taking a moment before reacting to frustrations. Balanced Triangles make outstanding leaders by combining strength and sensitivity.

Wavy Line Weaknesses

The open-mindedness of Wavy Lines can, if not kept in check, lead to indecisiveness. Setting goals and deadlines creates structure and aids in management. Even with spontaneity, organizing systems help prevent forgetting tasks. Their creative energy stays grounded by planning ahead.

Setting limits and saying no helps Wavy Lines avoid taking on too much. It's important for them to take care of themselves and communicate their needs while assisting others. Relationships improve when conflict avoidance turns into solution-focused conversations.

Improving impulsiveness and emotional sensitivity is necessary. Empathy grows and perspectives broaden when viewing from different angles. They become stronger when they see feedback as an opportunity to grow, not just criticism. Being disciplined and emotionally intelligent can help Wavy Lines turn their weaknesses into strengths.

Shape Recognition: Interaction

We learn how to recognize Shapes by observing how people behave and their nonverbal signals in different situations. They consistently reveal their strengths, weaknesses, and tendencies. Let's analyze more cues by interacting directly and taking a closer look.

The initial clues come from a handshake and greeting. During conversations, we observe their communication to learn from their words and body language. Strategic questions lead to revealing answers. The way interactions end can give clues about their Shape. We can also infer their temperament from voicemails and texts.

They reveal the core traits when we pay attention throughout the process. Every interaction, despite the uncertainty, improves our understanding of them. Gradually, we can quickly identify their core personalities and increase our understanding and connection.

What's the plan for doing this? A simple handshake and greeting is where it all begins.

Recognizing Their Shape by How They Shake Hands and Greet

How Circles Shake Hands and Greet

From the beginning, Circles show their warmth and empathy by the way they greet others. They shake hands with a gentle yet firm grip that's friendly but not pushy. They connect non-verbally, using hand gestures like clasping or touching shoulders. The strength of their eye contact suggests a shared purpose and unity.

They greet others with positivity and inclusivity. Frequent usage of names helps develop a sense of familiarity and recognition. If you want to start a conversation with Circles, ask about their interests and experiences. They create an environment where both parties feel safe to express their thoughts and emotions. They convey sincerity through their tone of voice and body language.

Circles excel in providing uplifting handshakes and greetings for both individuals involved. They use their touch and words to create meaningful connections. When you encounter a Circle, you feel as though you are seen, understood, and reinvigorated by the genuine bond that is established in those crucial initial moments. They create meaningful interactions by starting with a warm handshake and caring conversation.

How Squares Shake Hands and Greet

When Squares greet someone and shake hands, their precision and carefulness is immediately apparent. They shake hands in the usual way, with firmness and respect. It's designed to be both sturdy and comfortable. A quick glance into your eyes is followed by a polite look away to avoid awkwardness. At the perfect moment, they let go of your hand.

Squares exhibit a high level of professionalism when communicating. When communicating, they greet each other briefly and quickly get to the main point. Small talk is not their thing. Their focus is on adhering to the rules and ensuring that everyone comprehends the objectives. Their communication involves precise language.

Squares aim to convey their dependability and respectfulness through their greetings and handshakes. They focus on the task and spend little time chatting. Meeting them gives you the impression that they perceive your capabilities and how you can help accomplish tasks. The Square Shape facilitates practical interactions through a simple handshake and a coherent conversation.

How Triangles Shake Hands and Greet

The confidence and boldness of Triangles is clear in the way they greet others. They exhibit control with a firm and purposeful grip, while the motion of their handshake creates a sense of connection. Maintaining eye contact, they display their confidence and presence. They challenge others to match their energetic approach through their physical mannerisms.

Their greetings are goal-oriented and emphasize strength when they speak. They switch to using first names to create a sense of familiarity. Aligning their interests with important priorities and challenges happens swiftly. Their tone is both authoritative and attentive, showing they are in charge but also willing to work together.

Handshakes and greetings of Triangles convey their bigger picture mindset. Their touch and words convey a distinct purpose and direction. Their energy dynamic motivates and excites us to achieve. Through a firm handshake and confident conversation, Triangles provide a platform for objective-centered interactions.

How Wavy Lines Shake Hands and Greet

When Wavy Lines shake hands and greet others with energy, their warmth and creativity become apparent. Their handshake is a perfect blend of friendliness and professionalism. A two-handed clasp often follows their handshake, signifying a deep connection. Starting with eye contact, they allow their eyes to wander and gain inspiration from their surroundings.

Their speeches start with humor, lightness, and inclusive language. They inspire others to share their stories and passions, showing genuine interest. They create an environment where both sides can be open. Their tone is positive, intending to lift everyone's mood. Their instincts take the conversation in unpredictable directions.

Wavy Lines produce handshakes and greetings that generate excitement in new relationships. We feel optimistic because of their touch and words. Our meeting with them acknowledges us as humans, lifts us up, and motivates us to explore growth together. They establish a handshake that invites us and a compassionate way of speaking with them to foster open conversations.

Effective Approaches for Communicating with Each Shape

We greeted each other with a handshake. Now, we will investigate communication strategies tailored to connect with individuals effectively. If we understand someone's personality style, we can tailor our messaging and approach to best resonate with them. The marketing mistakes made by Bud Light showed that misunderstandings and a lack of trust occur when there's a mismatch. Conversely, matching communication to one's personality can establish a solid groundwork for developing rapport.

We'll discuss how to engage with each personality type based on their natural tendencies. You can create meaningful connections through smooth and sophisticated conversations by mastering this skill. When we combine personality styles and communication, we can unlock deep relationships.

Effective Approaches for Communicating with Circles

To connect with a Circle, you need to reciprocate their friendliness and expressiveness. Show a sincere interest in their experiences and feelings when you talk to them. Allow them room to tell their stories and actively listen to comprehend their perspective. Match their humor and enthusiasm, just like they do.

Being emotionally aware is crucial when dealing with Circles. Instead of trying to fix everything right away, show understanding if they talk about their problems. We shouldn't ignore or downplay their feelings. Show them you understand and that you're ready to help. Acknowledge their accomplishments publicly and privately to boost their confidence. Receive their kind words and gestures with grace.

When in conflicts, adopt a soft tone. Avoid being aggressive and focus on finding common ground and understanding each's goals. Harmony is significant. Use Circles' talent for mediation to handle varying opinions productively. Make sure they feel valued by regularly requesting their input while working together.

Effective Approaches for Communicating with Squares

Effective teamwork with detail-oriented and logical Squares requires organized communication and a structured setting. When talking with them, focus on clear and relevant topics and keep your messages concise. Avoid going off-topic and be precise when giving direction. Recognize that Squares prefer having time to gather important information before deciding. Provide them with context and data to support your ideas.

When you can, provide Squares with workflow processes that enhance efficiency. Clearly outline their responsibilities and set clear timelines. Establish well-organized systems for accessing resources and tracking progress. Offer positive feedback when Squares produce high-quality work, praising their thoroughness and consistency. Avoid introducing unnecessary complexity or ambiguity into their work environment.

Also, observe Squares' subtle emotional styles. Don't assume that their lack of expression means they don't have feelings. Observe their tone, wording, and body language for subtle cues instead. Respect their emotional boundaries, but still show that you care. When Squares confide in you about challenges, provide them with logical reassurance and empathy in private.

Effective Approaches for Communicating with Triangles

To work effectively with achievement-driven Triangles, it's important to grasp their goal-oriented focus. Discuss the desired outcomes and the direct correlation between efforts and results. Clarify their role in achieving outcomes. When they succeed, acknowledge it openly. Suggest feedback or ideas as a means of improvement, not as criticism. Make room for Triangles to share their ambitious ideas.

Be direct, clear, and open in your communication. Don't waste time with small talk, just clearly explain your requests. Establish precise time limits and boundaries to help Triangles decide promptly. If there's a change in priorities, give a reason and assist with the necessary adjustments. Commend the accomplishments of Triangle leaders in public, but offer private advice if required.

Consider the confidence and competitive spirit of Triangles as strengths. Encourage them to take calculated risks and be in control of their choices. Create openings for them to exhibit their expertise and take the helm of projects. Challenge them with tasks but monitor their stress levels and offer support.

Effective Approaches for Communicating with Wavy Lines

To effectively work with creative Wavy Lines, it's important to allow them the freedom to be imaginative and adaptable. They generate new solutions and explore possibilities during brainstorming sessions. Place boundaries on the project while allowing room for creative exploration. It's important to keep communicating regularly since their needs may change and strict rules could cause them frustration.

Promote open and non-judgmental communication by showing understanding and emotional support. Learn their thoughts by asking questions. Attempt to match their relaxed mannerisms and speech. Using humor, create an easygoing atmosphere that will make them comfortable to share their ideas. Encourage and praise creative solutions.

Build teamwork by forming teams composed of people with varying skills and personalities. The combination of varying strengths works well with Wavy Lines. They can change strategies effectively because of their adaptability. By utilizing their empathy, they can unite diverse groups. They show their abilities in team effort, idea generation, and reaching a consensus.

Recognizing Their Shape by Using Open-Ended Prompts

Chris Voss the Late-Night FM DJ

In his book "Never Split the Difference," Chris Voss, a former FBI negotiator, emphasizes the significance of utilizing open-ended prompts that can't be answered with a simple yes or no. Open-ended prompts help people share more about themselves. This approach plays a crucial role in how he communicates and negotiates. The usage of these prompts relaxes the environment, causing people to provide more detailed answers. Understanding this can reveal their true meaning and perspective. Voss' method has two benefits: understanding personality and building better connections. You can determine someone's personality traits through this approach. Instead of just asking, "What's your personality type?" use the following open-ended prompt:

"Tell me something I don't know about [topic]"

A Circle would talk about feelings or relationships related to the topic. They might share personal stories and connections instead of just facts. A Square would give specific details, facts that most people don't know, or technical knowledge about the topic. A Triangle can generate diverse opinions and unique analyses that offer a different perspective. They might want to impress with their different ways of thinking. A Wavy Line can respond with big or unusual ideas.

Because the prompt is open-ended, each Shape can answer it in their own way. Circles talk about people; Squares give facts; Triangles provoke thoughts; Wavy Lines use their imagination. This shows what each type naturally focuses on and how they like to communicate.

For example: "Tell me something I don't know about electric vehicles."

Circles would say, "From talking to some early EV owners, I was surprised by how the new ownership experience is bringing some communities of drivers together. People share charging stories and best practices that spark conversations you wouldn't have around gas cars."

Squares would say, "Most people don't realize that the cobalt content in lithium-ion batteries for EVs is miniscule, making up less than 5% of the cathode material. This counters myths about EV batteries using unsustainable cobalt sources."

Triangles would say, "While the EV hype focuses on sustainability, the underlying motivation for automakers is really the lucrative software and data opportunities that connected electric cars provide access to."

Wavy Lines would say, "I was thinking we could leverage EV battery technology in really creative ways, like pop-up charging stations or mobile power sources for off-grid outdoor events. The applications could go way beyond just powering vehicles."

Recognizing Their Shape by How They Disagree

Even when disagreements arise, Shapes show their inherent tendencies in how they deal with conflicts. They show their true selves when they discuss differences, seek solutions, and try to keep things positive during arguments. By observing how each Shape reacts to tension, you can gather more information about them. Understanding how Shapes handle disagreements gives you more insight into their character. This guides you in how to speak to them or find a middle ground more effectively based on what's important to them. In this section, we'll look at how Shapes approach disagreements when they express their true selves. But first, a quick discussion about the photograph that broke the internet.

The Dress

In 2015, a viral disagreement broke out in response to a seemingly innocuous photograph of a dress. While the dress was actually blue and black, people couldn't agree if it was white and gold or blue and black. This color confusion caused heated debates on social media.

This situation shows how the lighting and our unique ways of seeing things can make us see the same picture differently. Our brains usually figure out the color by looking at what's around it. Some brains thought the dress was white and gold, while others saw it as blue and black.

Images of the dress spread quickly online and became a symbol of how subjective our realities can be. The power of this perceived illusion can be explained by science. It opened up discussions on how our location and the mechanics of our eyes can influence what we see. It showed that each person's point of view affects how they perceive the world. A simple picture made us realize that we all see things in our own way.

This famous illusion made everyone think about how what we see can change based on who we are and what's around us. People argued about how our identity and surroundings shape what we think is real. The dress showed how even when something seems clear, people can still understand it in really different ways because we're all unique.

So, what were we looking at? In the end, no one was seeing it right or wrong; it was simply an issue of perception and how we were built. We all agreed to disagree.

How Circles Disagree With You

When Circles disagree, they focus on resolving issues through open dialogue and finding ways they can agree. They share their opinions gently, trying not to hurt anyone. They start by establishing a mutual understanding between both parties, so that they can have a clearer view of the other's point of view. If they don't see eye-to-eye, they use "I feel" statements to explain how they see things.

If things get worse, Circles change how they talk to keep things peaceful. They recognize the merits of both positions, demonstrating that each has worth. They show that even if they disagree, they still care about the same goals and values. This helps them find a middle ground. They also come up with creative ideas to make everyone happy.

Circles care about the relationship, and they believe it can withstand conflict. With kindness, they make things right by focusing on how they're connected and how they can grow together. Circles argue thoughtfully, saying what they think but staying kind. They show that even when they disagree, they care about each other's feelings.

How Squares Disagree With You

When Squares have disagreements, they try to keep things logical and focused on finding solutions. They explain their reasons clearly and back up their opinions with facts. They break down the areas of disagreement clearly to get to the main issues. Squares come up with ideas for compromise based on the facts, and they want solutions that are fair and sensible.

If things get emotional, they'll recognize feelings, but bring the conversation back to practical steps. Squares can see both sides, but they care more about solving the problem efficiently. They come up with plans to fix the issues and say what needs to happen next.

Squares stay focused on solving the problem, not blaming the person. They believe they can find a fair solution by staying calm. They disagree with maturity and respect the other person's viewpoint. Squares handle disagreements carefully, saying what they think but staying reasonable. They show how important it is to be fair and do what's right, even when there are differences.

How Triangles Disagree With You

When Triangles don't agree, they state their opinion directly and give reasons that make sense. They express their views honestly but also respectfully, trying to make sure everyone understands. They explain why their way is best for reaching the goals everyone shares. When there's a difference, they try to find the best parts of each side and put them together for the best solution.

If things get more heated, they bring the talk back to what everyone wants to achieve and practical answers. Triangles can see good points on both sides, but they want to figure out what's the best overall. They inspire everyone to recognize their role in achieving success as a team. Their shared drive and determination can overcome disagreements.

Triangles focus on the bigger picture, believing that it takes the combined efforts of a team to successfully address and resolve any problems that arise. They disagree but still show respect for the individual. When dealing with disagreements, they prioritize the bigger goal while expressing their beliefs. They show how to aim for greatness even when there are differences.

How Wavy Lines Disagree With You

When Wavy Lines don't agree, they try to figure out what's really bothering each side. They share how they feel in a caring way and make sure not to ignore how others feel. Wavy Lines consider everyone's interest, even when they see things differently. If they don't agree, they try to see how the situation could make them all grow and think in new ways.

If things get worse, they switch the discussion to imagine the best outcome. Wavy Lines can see good things on both sides and say what's important. They make everyone think about how they're all human and can come up with new solutions that help everyone.

Wavy Lines care about the relationship and think it can handle disagreements. They handle disagreements by saying what they feel while still being kind. They show how to make things right by being open, using their imagination, and caring about each other.

Recognizing Their Shape by How They Disengage

The end of a conversation can give important hints about someone's real Shape. When people finish talking, their natural tendencies show in how they sum up the main points, show gratitude, move on to the next steps, and say goodbye. Each Shape has their own unique way of wrapping things up based on who they are. Observing how different people end conversations can provide valuable clues into identifying their Shape. Getting good at recognizing this adds another level of understanding.

How Circles Disengage From Conversations

When they're wrapping up conversations, Circles make sure they leave things that show they want to keep talking later. They go over the important topics to show they were really listening and to point out what they agreed on. By discussing what could happen next, they show their commitment to maintaining the relationship. They also express their appreciation for the pleasant conversation and knowledge shared between them.

Circles get personal when it's time to say goodbye. They talk about how much they enjoy connecting and getting to know each other better. Names are frequently used to make it feel special. They extend an invitation to the other person to get together again soon and continue developing their relationship. They might even give you a warm hug or pat on the shoulder to show they care.

How Squares Disengage From Conversations

Squares try to make things neat and organized when they're finishing up interactions. They go over what they talked about and decided on in a structured way to make sure everyone understands. They set up plans to keep things going in the future. People receive acknowledgment and appreciation for their time and effort.

When it's time to say goodbye, they focus on what got done and what needs to happen next. They use clear and direct language to show who's responsible for what. They remind everyone to finish their tasks and keep their promises. To show their hard work and progress, they may shake hands.

How Triangles Disengage From Conversations

Triangles make sure everyone knows what's going to happen next and who's responsible when they're wrapping up talks. They clearly state what the plan is and what each person needs to do. To inspire everyone, they reiterate their big goals. They also thank the team for their hard work and show they believe in reaching the goals.

When it's time to say goodbye, they keep the motivation going. The emphasis is on the progress achieved and the need to keep pushing forward. Strong language is used to show their determination. They encourage people to focus on the bigger picture, even while performing daily tasks. To keep everyone motivated, they may give pats on the back.

How Wavy Lines Disengage From Conversations

When they're ending conversations, Wavy Lines try to leave you feeling inspired and ready for more. They talk about the cool ideas and creative thoughts that came up, and they show how those ideas could lead to exciting things in the future. They express their gratitude for the creative vibes and fresh perspective.

Wavy Lines make you feel you've been part of something special when it's time to say goodbye. They talk about how fun it was to connect and share ideas. They use words that make everyone feel included. Together, they invite you to keep exploring. Sometimes they might even give you a friendly hug to show they care.

Recognizing Their Shape by Their Voicemail Message

Let's listen to their voicemail messages.

How to Recognize a Circle by Their Voicemail Message

"Hi there! You've reached [Name] and I deeply apologize for not being available to answer your call. I do want to hear what you have to say because your call means a lot to me. So, leave me a message of any length with a bit of your bright energy, and I promise to get back to you as soon as I can. Let's stay connected and make some great things happen together. Have a fantastic day!"

The Tells:

Warm Greeting: The message starts with a friendly and cheerful "Hi there!" This shows a Circle's natural inclination to create a welcoming and positive atmosphere in interactions.

Apologetic and Considerate Tone: The speaker offers a sincere apology for missing the call, which reflects the Circle's sensitivity to others' feelings and their desire to maintain harmony, even in situations where they can't immediately respond.

Valuing Connection: The message emphasizes that the caller's input is important and valued, aligning with a Circle's strong focus on relationships and the desire to foster connections.

Encouraging Interaction: The speaker encourages the caller to leave a message with their "bright energy," showcasing the Circle's enthusiasm for shared experiences and emotional engagement.

Promise of Prompt Response: The speaker assures the caller that they will get back to them as soon as possible, showing a Circle's commitment to maintaining communication and ensuring others feel heard.

Teamwork and Positivity: The message ends with an invitation to "make great things happen together." This collaborative approach and optimistic outlook resonate with a Circle's tendency to promote teamwork and encourage positive outcomes.

Well-Wishing: The voicemail concludes with a cheerful "Have a fantastic day," which reflects the Circle's genuine care for the well-being and happiness of others.

The voicemail displays traits of a Circle personality, including being friendly, empathetic, relationship-focused, connection-driven, positive, and committed to communication.

How to Recognize a Square by Their Voicemail Message

"Hi, you've reached [Name] at [Number]. I cannot take your call right now. Please speak clearly and leave your name, number, the date and time you called, and a detailed message after the tone. I will promptly return your call within 24 hours. If you would prefer to contact me via email, my email address is [email]. Thank you."

The Tells:

Clear Instructions: The message is structured and provides clear instructions on what the caller needs to do. Square personalities are known for their organized and methodical approach, and they prefer communication that is structured and straightforward.

Details and Specifics: The message requests specific details, such as the caller's name, number, date, and time of the call. Square personalities value precision and accuracy, and they appreciate when information is presented in a detailed manner.

Prompt Response: The message assures the caller that the call will be returned within 24 hours. Square personalities prioritize efficiency and timely communication, which is reflected in the commitment to respond quickly.

Alternative Contact Method: The message offers an alternative way of contact by providing an email address. Square personalities often think ahead and provide backup plans, which is demonstrated here by offering an email option.

Formal Tone: The language used in the message is formal and professional, reflecting the careful communication style associated with Square personalities.

A Square personality's characteristics match the voicemail's emphasis on explicit instructions, specific details, prompt response, alternatives, and a formal tone.

How to Recognize a Triangle by Their Voicemail Message

"Hello, you've reached [Name]. While I'm currently unavailable to take your call, your message is important to me. Please leave your name, number, and a detailed explanation of the reason for your call. I appreciate clear and concise information and will review your message and respond accordingly. I'm committed to addressing your concerns or inquiries as promptly as possible. Thank you for getting in touch."

The Tells:

Warm and Welcoming: The message begins with a polite and friendly tone, showing a desire to establish a positive connection. Triangle personalities often excel in building rapport and creating a welcoming atmosphere.

Acknowledges Importance: The message emphasizes the importance of the caller's message. Triangle personalities are people-oriented and value interpersonal connections, trying to express genuine interest in others.

Clear Communication: The message requests specific information—name, number, and reason for the call—demonstrating the Triangle's preference for clear and concise communication. Triangles value getting to the point and appreciate when others do the same.

Commitment to Resolution: The message assures the caller that the concerns or inquiries will be addressed promptly. Triangles are goal-oriented and take on responsibilities seriously, aiming to resolve issues efficiently.

Professionalism: The language used is professional and courteous, reflecting the Triangle's inclination towards respectful communication.

Structured Approach: The message follows a structured format, including an introduction, request for information, and assurance of prompt response. Triangles often appreciate organized and well-defined processes.

The voicemail message aligns with the traits of a Triangle personality: warmth, importance, clear communication, commitment, professionalism, and a structured approach.

How to Recognize a Wavy Line by Their Voicemail Message

"Hey there, this is [Name]. I'm not able to pick up the phone right now, but I'm excited to hear what you have to say! Drop me a message with your name, number, and any cool thoughts or ideas you want to share. Feel free to get creative or tell me something interesting. I'll be back to you soon with a smile and maybe even a wild idea of my own. Thanks for leaving your message, and let's keep the good vibes going!"

The Tells:

Friendly and Casual Tone: The message begins with a laid-back and friendly greeting, aligning with the Wavy Line's approachable and easygoing nature. They often start interactions in an informal manner.

Expresses Excitement: The message conveys genuine enthusiasm and excitement about hearing from the caller. Wavy Lines are known for their enthusiastic and energetic approach to communication, often showing genuine interest in others' ideas.

Encourages Creativity: The message encourages the caller to share creative thoughts or ideas. Wavy Lines value creativity and originality and enjoy engaging in imaginative and unique discussions.

Positive and Upbeat: The message maintains a positive and upbeat tone throughout, reflecting the Wavy Line's preference for maintaining a positive atmosphere and fostering good vibes.

Open to Diverse Conversations: The message welcomes a range of topics and invites the caller to "get creative" or "tell something interesting." Wavy Lines enjoy exploring a variety of subjects and are open to free-flowing conversations.

Potential for Spontaneity: The mention of coming back with a "wild idea of my own" suggests the Wavy Line's inclination towards spontaneous and unconventional thinking.

Non-Formal Language: The use of phrases like "Hey there" and "Drop me a message" reflects the Wavy Line's informal and personable communication style.

Maintains Positivity: The message concludes with a positive note, encouraging the continuation of good vibes. Wavy Lines often prioritize maintaining a positive and friendly atmosphere in their interactions.

The voicemail's non-formal language, encouragement of creativity, and excitement align with a Wavy Line personality.

Recognizing Their Shape by Their Text Messages

Let's text them.

How to Recognize a Circle by Their Text Messages

Here's an example of a text message that reflects the communication style of a Circle personality:

> Hey there! How's your day going? 😊 Just wanted to check in and see how you're doing. Remember that coffee shop we talked about? I heard they have a new latte flavor, and I thought it could be fun to try it together sometime this week. Let me know if that works for you! If not, we can definitely find another time that suits both of us. Take care and talk soon! 💫

In this text, you can see the warmth, friendliness, and focus on building a connection that are characteristic of a Circle personality. Circles use emojis, ask about your day, suggest social activities, and have a positive and inclusive tone when they communicate.

How to Recognize a Square by Their Text Messages

Here's an example of a text message that reflects the communication style of a Square personality:

> Good day! I hope this message finds you well. I wanted to discuss the upcoming project we're collaborating on. Could you please confirm the timeline for the next phase? It's essential that we adhere to the schedule to maintain efficiency. Additionally, if you could provide a brief update on the research, you've conducted so far, that would be greatly appreciated. Thank you for your attention to detail and dedication to our goals.

In this text, you can observe the structured and formal approach characteristic of a Square personality. They focus the message on the project's details, timelines, and efficient communication. Square's communication style uses formal language, makes straightforward requests, and emphasizes organization and professionalism.

How to Recognize a Triangle by Their Text Messages

Here's an example of a text message that reflects the communication style of a Triangle personality:

> Hi! I've been researching different strategies for our project, and I think I've found a few that could really work. Let's meet up and discuss them in detail. I value your insights and I'm sure together we can come up with a solid plan. Looking forward to bouncing ideas off each other and taking action!

This text message shows the Triangle's tendency to be proactive and results-driven. The focus is on finding practical solutions and taking decisive steps forward. Using phrases like "discuss them in detail," "solid plan," and "taking action" reflects the Triangle's preference for concrete actions and strategic thinking. Valuing the other person's insights shows an appreciation for collaboration and teamwork.

How to Recognize a Wavy Line by Their Text Messages

This says:

"Hello! How about grabbing a burger and hitting the beach this weekend? We could have a great time in the sun with some music!"

If All Else Fails...

Scooby-Do It

Sometimes, even after careful observation and engaging conversations, deciphering someone's Shape remains a mystery. It's not uncommon for certain personalities to defy easy categorization within the framework of the four Shapes. In these instances, "Scooby-Do" it.

Here's how: Ask the person to draw the four Shapes on a sheet of paper and then, without overthinking, place a check mark next to the one that resonates with them the most. If paper isn't available, simply ask them to envision the Shapes in their mind and pick the one they most relate to. While they're doing this, take a moment to predict which Shape they'll choose. Trust your intuition and make your prediction.

What follows is a captivating exchange, regardless of whether your prediction aligns with their choice. The discussion that unfolds is rich and meaningful, shedding light on their personality in ways that extend beyond a simple guess.

Transformative Growth

PART 3: Beyond the Cover: The "Hidden Guru" Shape

Perhaps it was ego, or maybe genuine curiosity, but I decided to give his advice a try. To my astonishment, the difference in my squat form and engagement was palpable. This misjudged yard elf had unknowingly provided a key to unlock a better glute workout.

Shape Transformation

Welcome to the last chapter. Here, we will delve into the essence of Shape transformation. We'll start by looking at your secondary Shape—an essential aspect that adds depth to your self-discovery. Then we'll explore the temptation to change Shapes and how our personalities mature. We'll discuss the power of surrounding yourself with dissenters, those who challenge your perspective. We'll also acknowledge the limitations of the Shapes PIM. And as we reach the end, we will discuss your three new superpowers.

Your Secondary Shape

When exploring personality Shapes, it's important to understand that you have a primary and a secondary one. Your primary Shape represents your core traits and tendencies, shaping a significant part of your identity. The secondary Shape adds a dynamic layer to your personality that shines in different situations.

Think of your primary Shape as the cornerstone of your personality puzzle. It's the dominant force that influences how you naturally perceive and interact with the world around you. But life is rarely static, and circumstances can prompt different sides of you to emerge. This is where the secondary Shape comes into play.

Your secondary Shape may show up when you face challenges or stress. It's like having an alternate lens through which you perceive and engage with your surroundings. Your secondary Shape may not be as noticeable as your primary one, but it still can influence your behavior and reactions.

Imagine you're primarily a Circle, characterized by your social and optimistic nature. In complex projects that require planning and detail, your secondary Triangle traits may be critical. You analyze data, thinking about different perspectives, and creating a complete plan, which is more in line with the Triangle Shape.

If you're a Square, you might experience secondary Wavy Line characteristics in social situations. You could surprise yourself by being creative and talking spontaneously at a party.

By accepting your secondary Shape, you gain a wider range of resources to deal with life's intricacies. It allows you to adapt and respond in ways that harmonize with the situation at hand. Acknowledging this secondary layer can increase your self-awareness and strengths.

The Temptation to Change Shapes

Trying to act in ways that don't match your natural personality can hurt your emotions and relationships. When you force yourself to hide your real tendencies and pretend to be someone else, it often leads to inner stress and confusion. You might feel disconnected from who you truly are and not find much fulfillment.

This kind of pretending also messes up how you communicate and connect with others. When your actual personality doesn't match the one you're showing, it confuses people. It's hard to build trust when others feel you're not being genuine. And when your goals don't match what drives you, they lose their importance.

Going against your strengths can make you less efficient and motivated. What comes naturally to one person might drain another. It's tiring pretending to be someone else. Instead of finding success, you'll end up feeling frustrated. Growing is important, but not by giving up your natural talents.

When you don't stay true to yourself, it can negatively impact your happiness, relationships, performance, and self-image. Embracing your true personality is liberating and helps you develop skills that match it. By understanding your authentic nature, your confidence will soar.

Stede Bonnet

The story of Stede Bonnet, known as the Gentleman Pirate, serves as a powerful example. Despite being a wealthy landowner from Barbados with no sailing or fighting skills, Bonnet arbitrarily decided to become a pirate. He bought a ship, hired a crew, and set off on a pirate's life, which was completely contrary to his previous lifestyle.

This turned out to be a disaster, much like trying to fit into the wrong personality Shape. Because of Bonnet's lack of knowledge about sailing, he suffered embarrassing defeats. Ignoring his responsibilities harmed his reputation and sense of self. Opting for violence instead of his usual way of life cut him off from society. He faced legal consequences for his criminal actions. Worst of all, this failed attempt at changing who he was brought him no happiness; he only felt disconnected and unsuccessful.

Bonnet's story teaches us about the heavy costs of not being true to ourselves. Just as his failed piracy led to ruin, forcing ourselves to behave against our true nature has negative outcomes. Suppressing our natural talents steals away our happiness and damages our relationships. But accepting ourselves gives us the freedom to build on our strengths and grow. His story teaches us that some personalities just won't mesh, and it's better to be true to ourselves than to pretend otherwise.

Shapeshifting and the Evolution of Personality

Personality isn't just one thing that stays the same. It's more like a shape that can change and shift, a bit like how a person might change their behavior, feelings, and thoughts over time. These changes are influenced by a combination of internal and external factors. Life events, experiences, and interactions with the world can all make these shifts happen. This illustrates that personalities aren't set in stone; they can change.

Shapeshifting occurs when a person adapts to their ever-changing circumstances. Major life events like getting a new job, starting a family, or achieving personal goals, can cause people to alter their behavior to fit in with their current surroundings. Shapeshifting isn't just about changing on the outside; it also involves modifying one's mindset to effectively adapt to different situations.

It's important to realize that Shapeshifting isn't the same for everyone. Some people go through big changes, while others have smaller shifts. It depends on how well someone can adjust, how they cope with things, and how important the event is to them. When we see personalities aren't set in stone, we think differently about people. We see they can adapt and change, which makes us rethink how they connect with themselves and the world.

Wanted: Devil's Advocate

When we use personality models like Shapes, there's a danger we need to watch out for: ignoring or avoiding certain types of personalities. Ori Brafman's work in "Sway" covers an essential topic: dissenters. He says that people who disagree with the group can be valuable, even though they might annoy everyone at first. These different opinions can make the final decisions better by stopping the group from only thinking one way.

This idea applies to different personality types, too. Instead of pushing away certain Shapes, we should listen to them. Engaging with people who challenge our ideas can lead to more meaningful conversations instead of just hearing what we want to hear. Just like those who disagree make us think harder, having different personality Shapes gives us a mix of ideas.

Each Shape has its own strengths, and when we bring all those strengths together, it's like weaving a colorful pattern. Including everyone may lead to disagreements, but it benefits us all. When we include many people, not just the ones we like, we can talk and make choices more thoughtfully. Brafman says that embracing the diversity of Shapes helps us reach our potential. Moving forward happens when we're open to different ideas, not when everyone is the same.

Acknowledgment of Limitations

The Shapes Personality Identification Model, while insightful and useful, also has its limitations. It's important to be aware of these aspects to have a well-rounded understanding:

Simplicity and Generalization: The model may oversimplify human personalities by categorizing people into just four Shapes. People are unique and complex, and categorizing them into four Shapes may overlook important differences.

Fixed Labels: Assigning someone a specific Shape might create a fixed label that doesn't fully capture the dynamic nature of their personality. People can evolve, change, and adapt over time, making it challenging to confine them to a single Shape throughout their lives.

Limited Scope: The model focuses on four Shapes, which might not encompass the entirety of human personality traits and behaviors. People who don't fit into a specific category might be hard to assess accurately.

Cultural and Contextual Variations: Cultural backgrounds, upbringing, and environmental factors can influence personality. The model might not fully account for these variations, leading to misinterpretations or misunderstandings across different cultural contexts.

Overlooking Complexity: Human behavior is often a blend of various traits and tendencies, which can't always be neatly categorized into distinct Shapes. The model might struggle to capture the intricate interplay between different aspects of personality.

Bias and Stereotyping: Relying solely on the Shapes model can lead to oversimplification and stereotyping. Labeling people by their Shape can lead to unfair judgments.

Self-Fulfilling Prophecy: Once someone assigns individuals a Shape, they might start conforming to the traits associated with that Shape, even if those traits don't completely align with their authentic selves. This can lead to a self-fulfilling prophecy where individuals mold their behavior to fit the Shape's description.

Lack of Scientific Validation: The Shapes model is a conceptual framework rather than a scientifically validated personality assessment tool. Its accuracy and reliability might vary, and it lacks the empirical backing of more established personality theories.

Personal Growth: While the model can provide insights into understanding oneself and others, it might not offer a comprehensive guide for personal growth and development. Individuals might need additional tools and strategies to address their unique needs and aspirations.

We need to be aware of the limitations of the Shapes Personality Identification Model despite its valuable insights. We can achieve a more complete understanding of human behavior and relationships by combining various personality theories and taking individual complexity into account.

Your New Superpowers

Proficiency in recognizing Shapes gives us three remarkable powers: enhanced self-awareness, enhanced communication, empathy, and strengthened relationships and teams.

Superpower #1: Enhanced Self-Awareness

Understanding your primary Shape is like holding up a mirror to your own tendencies. It's a tool that lets you see patterns in your behavior, motivations, and emotional responses. This self-awareness allows you to align your actions with your values and make more informed decisions. You recognize blind spots and areas where you can grow.

As you delve into the different Shapes and their characteristics, you understand your own personality in a deeper way. You might find traits that resonate with you and traits that challenge you. You can explore and embrace your authentic self without being judged. Personal growth comes from setting personality-matching goals and developing strength-based skills.

Superpower #2: Enhanced Communication and Empathy

Unlocking the world of Shapes isn't just about recognizing personalities; it's also a powerful tool for enhancing communication and empathy. When we grasp the Shapes framework, a whole new level of understanding unfolds, enriching our interactions with others.

Imagine having a decoder for communication styles—that's what understanding Shapes provides. Each Shape has its own distinct way of conveying thoughts and feelings. Squares like direct and logical conversations, while Circles prefer optimistic and relational ones. By tailoring our messages to match these preferences, we create connections that resonate.

Recognizing Shapes helps us understand the unique viewpoints and challenges of others. When we comprehend why a Triangle might prioritize urgency or a Wavy Line embraces creativity, compassion grows. This empathy forms the foundation of strong relationships and harmonious teamwork.

If we use our understanding of Shapes when communicating, conflicts can transform into meaningful discussions. We reframe criticism, considering how each Shape receives feedback. This fosters a culture of openness and mutual respect. Shapes can help us find common ground and keep relationships strong.

Superpower #3: Strengthened Relationships and Teams

Understanding Shapes goes beyond self-awareness; it has the incredible power to transform the way we relate to others and work in teams. Imagine a puzzle where each piece is unique, yet together they create a complete picture. Understanding the dynamics of Shapes can help us connect with people better.

In relationships, knowing the Shapes of those around us allows us to communicate more effectively. We can tailor our interactions to resonate with their preferences, making them feel understood and valued. For instance, if someone has a Circle Shape, they appreciate warmth and connection. So, by adopting a friendly and enthusiastic approach, we create an environment where they thrive. When we adapt our communication styles based on Shapes, misunderstandings dwindle and empathy flourishes.

Understanding Shapes leads to more effective conflict resolution. When we recognize the Shapes at play, we understand how each person approaches conflicts. A Triangle might offer strategic solutions, while a Wavy Line brings creative alternatives. When we accept diverse viewpoints, disputes become chances for development.

The impact of Shape understanding extends to teams as well. Picture a sports team where each player brings a unique skill to the game. Similarly, in a workplace or any group setting, individuals of different Shapes offer diverse strengths. A Circle may excel at fostering camaraderie, while a Square thrives at organization. Acknowledging and using these strengths helps teams to be versatile and better equipped to tackle obstacles.

Epilogue

Antonio

Over time, as our interactions became less about unsolicited advice and more about genuine conversations, I discovered the layers behind his eccentric facade. He wasn't just a gym enthusiast; he was deeply passionate about helping others realize their potential. Beyond the gym, I learned he was a doting father to two young girls and had carved out a niche for himself as a freelance fitness instructor.

The man I had prematurely labeled as a simple annoyance had reshaped my gym experience and, in many ways, my perspective on snap judgments. Every interaction with Antonio served as a lesson—a reminder that the stories and depths of people often lie hidden beneath their outward "Shape."

Selah[1]

The end of this work is a good place for us to pause, reflect, and prepare.

Knowing our audience and communicating effectively are crucial for better connection and interaction. We've learned about different models from the past and present that have given us insights into human behavior. And by using personality models, we can prevent misunderstandings.

As we progressed through this book, the lessons became clearer.

The Shapes Personality Identification Model has been our guide. It improved our understanding of human actions. We've learned how to identify each

---

[1] "Selah" is a term that appears frequently in the Hebrew Bible, particularly in the Book of Psalms. Its exact meaning is uncertain, but it's often interpreted as a musical or liturgical direction indicating a pause or a moment of reflection. It's used to prompt the reader or singer to stop, ponder, and absorb the meaning of what has just been said.

personality Shape in different situations. Shapes' analysis exposed insights into human behavior.

By understanding what we're looking at, we can communicate better, adapt more easily, and work more efficiently with others.

We can take this wisdom with us. We can apply what we've learned in our interactions, relationships, and life experiences. Let's appreciate our differences and use Shapes to connect.

What are you looking at? It's not a wall, a spear, a snake, a tree, or a fan. It's an elephant.

Not Just Another Filipino Male in Line

And so, who am I? I'm like you. I am a work in progress.

In the past, I found myself surrounded by people who I perceived as idiots. I believed they lacked the foresight and efficiency that I possessed.

However, with time and introspection, I realized these people were not idiots at all.

It was simple. I was a Triangle, and they were not.

Afterword

The 9-foot Trestle Table, the Raven, and Fabio

Craftsmanship, whether it be in woodworking or writing, follows a familiar path. In my spare time, I'm a better-than-average woodworker. The construction of this book mirrors the approach I take when crafting larger pieces, like a 9-foot trestle table.

The first step is to translate a vision onto paper. I identify and secure the materials and then proceed to the workshop to start the process. Next comes the actual construction phase. The last steps include sanding with grits ranging from 80 to 220, then staining, and painting. Once finished, I take a step back and stare at it, questioning how to make it better. Did I miss something?

I'm staring at it. It feels like there was more to say on the topic, maybe even enough for a second volume. What I included in these pages is enough. Enough to help you be better than directionally accurate. And how rude would it be for me to insult your intelligence? Consider this gem from Glengarry Glen Ross: "Hey, let me buy you a pack of gum. I'll show you how to chew it."

The over-thinker says, "I'm done staring. It's enough."

In constructing this work, I faced the challenge of catering to all four different Shapes. Just as Edgar Allan Poe dissected his creative process in "The Philosophy of Composition," I began with the effect in mind. Not just the words on the page, but the emotions they would evoke.

I wanted you to walk away feeling that the content was appealing, the presentation was engaging, and above all, the information was helpful. I hope you found exactly that—helpfulness.

But even before all that, how did I convince you to pick up this book? That, too, required thought. In my mind's eye, my audience is comprised of those stuck in airport delays, seeking something substantial yet manageable to read. Metaphorically, they just wanted a healthy snack, not a seven-course meal. This is that.

And something that they could engage with without feeling guilt or shame. I envisioned a book that you could openly read without embarrassment—more "Atomic Habits" than "Apache Heartbeat" (whose cover features Fabio coyly holding a ravishing woman while their windswept hair blows in distinctly opposite directions). I may be wrong.

The information's helpfulness was always the primary goal.

In the end, the ideas in this book aimed to bring together form and function, appeal, and utility. It's been a journey to ensure that what you hold in your hands resonates with your needs and aspirations, and that, to me, is a worthy legacy.

Acknowledgements

Kimberly Enders

I'm very grateful to my colleague Kimberly Enders for her support and guidance in shaping this book. Kimberly, you are the "Super-Nudger", fearlessly challenging me by holding up a mirror to my actions and words. You kick-started this transformative journey with just five words over a cup of coffee in Mt. Clemens, Michigan: "You're all talk, San Juan." And when I needed a reality check on my priorities, you didn't hesitate to offer five more words: "You're being greedy, San Juan." Your words transcended mere accountability; they were infused with your distinctive blend of honesty and encouragement. Your influence has left an indelible mark on these pages, and for that, I am profoundly thankful.

Grace Buffa

I would like to express my sincere gratitude to my great friend Grace Buffa, whose influence on this work is immeasurable. Grace, even when it meant forfeiting your own time, you kindly let me soak up your knowledge. Your extraordinary capacity to make room for other people to express themselves has been a priceless gift. You've never told me to be a better listener; instead, you just showed me, and I just copied you. Your unassuming power and unfailing support have been a beacon of hope all along the way. Grace, I'm grateful for your tremendous influence. Not only has your presence influenced this book but also how I view relationships and effective communication.

The Woj

To my unwavering friend, Mike Wojcik — our bond goes beyond driving ranges, shared laughs on the golf course, and fantasy football side bets. Beyond that and the achievements of our remarkable children lies a foundation of shared values and authentic friendship. I may not mention you on every page of this book, but your impact is present in the lessons and wisdom shared. You're not just a golfing companion, a fantasy football commissioner, and an amazing father; you're a confidant and the truest of friends. Your imprint on this work, though silent, mirrors the immense impact you've made on my life. Thank you, Mike, for simply being you.

Alex and Adonis San Juan

To my brothers, poster children for Circles and Squares. You've been the unbreakable foundation on which my life rests. Without you, I am not complete; I am merely a fragment of the whole. All my trophies and scars—you've been there, front-row-center, with unending love and unwavering acceptance. As I pen down these stories within the pages of this book, I realize they are more than narratives. They are the longest and most heartfelt thank you ever offered in Filipino history. Your presence has shaped every word and every thought, and for that, I am forever grateful.

Resources and Further Reading

For a deeper exploration into the facets of personality, human behavior, and the art of understanding, the following books have been selected to complement the themes presented in this work:

"LIFE WOULD BE EASY IF IT WEREN'T FOR OTHER PEOPLE" BY CONNIE PODESTA (2017)

Complements the insights provided in "Navigating Personalities and Relationships through Shapes," offers a richer exploration of human behavior and communication, enhancing the depth of understanding on the intricacies of interpersonal dynamics, and resonates deeply with the principles of the Shapes program.

"READING PEOPLE: HOW SEEING THE WORLD THROUGH THE LENS OF PERSONALITY CHANGES EVERYTHING" BY ANNE BOGEL (2017)

Complements the foundational understanding introduced in "Building Foundations," enhancing depth on the significance of understanding various personality frameworks and their real-world applications.

"TALKING TO STRANGERS: WHAT WE SHOULD KNOW ABOUT THE PEOPLE WE DON'T KNOW" BY MALCOLM GLADWELL (2019)

Echoes the themes in "The Consequences of Getting It Wrong," emphasizing the complexities and potential pitfalls of reading and misunderstanding personalities.

"THE PERSONALITY BROKERS: THE STRANGE HISTORY OF MYERS-BRIGGS AND THE BIRTH OF PERSONALITY TESTING: BY MERVE EMRE (2019)

Resonates with the historical perspective provided in "Personality Identification Models: Past to Present," giving you deeper insight into the development and influence of the Myers-Briggs Type Indicator.

"WIRED THAT WAY: A COMPREHENSIVE GUIDE TO UNDERSTANDING AND MAXIMIZING YOUR

Personality Type: by Marita Littauer and Florence Littauer (2006)

Aligns with the exploration of personality traits and temperaments in "Shapes Personality Identification Model: Traits, Temperaments, and Effectiveness," offering an expansive guide on various personality types.

"The Four Tendencies: The Indispensable Personality Profiles that Reveal How to Make Your Life Better (and Other People's Lives Better, too)" by Gretchen Rubin (2017)

Enriches the discussion in "The Connection Between Shapes and The Four Temperaments" by presenting another lens through which to categorize and understand personalities.

"The Road Back to You: An Enneagram Journey to Self-Discovery" by Ian Morgan Cron and Suzanne Stabile (2016)

Adds another dimension to the exploration of personality models, enabling you to draw comparisons and contrasts with the Shapes Personality Identification Model.

"Captivate: The Science of Succeeding with People" by Vanessa Van Edwards (2018)

Enhances the sections on recognizing Shapes, especially in observational contexts, by introducing techniques to intuitively understand and connect with different personalities.

"Presence: Bringing Your Boldest Self to Your Biggest Challenges" by Amy Cuddy (2018)

Provides depth to the "Recognizing Shapes by Behavioral Patterns and Body Language," section, emphasizing the potency of body language and its role in understanding personalities.

"Surrounded by Idiots: The Four Types of Human Behavior and How to Effectively Communicate with Each in Business (and in Life)" by Thomas Erikson (2020)

Extends the concepts in "Effective Approaches for Communicating with Each Shape," providing you with practical strategies for tailored communication based on personality types.

"NEVER SPLIT THE DIFFERENCE: NEGOTIATING AS IF YOUR LIFE DEPENDED ON IT" BY CHRIS VOSS (2016)

Enhances the insights presented in "Effective Approaches for Communicating with Each Shape," providing advanced negotiation techniques and the psychology behind effective communication in high-stakes scenarios.

"QUIET: THE POWER OF INTROVERTS IN A WORLD THAT CAN'T STOP TALKING" BY SUSAN CAIN (2013)

Offers a deepened perspective on the spectrum of personalities, enhancing the discussion around recognizing Shapes in diverse settings and the importance of accommodating different temperaments.

"SWAY: THE IRRESISTIBLE PULL OF IRRATIONAL BEHAVIOR" BY ORI BRAFMAN AND ROM BRAFMAN (2009)

Relates to the transformative growth and shapeshifting sections, offering a deep dive into the psychological forces behind irrational behaviors.

"THE RAVEN, AND THE PHILOSOPHY OF COMPOSITION" BY EDGAR ALLAN POE (2015)

While not directly tied to personality identification, this classic piece reinforces the meticulous nature of understanding and categorizing, mirroring the deliberate approach required to effectively recognize and navigate personalities.

Shape Index

Mastering the content of this book requires a solid grasp of the dynamics between the four Shapes in various situations. This index makes it easy for you to find information on Shapes and interaction styles.

Circle

Square

Triangle

Wavy Line

Coming Soon

In the early pages of this guide, I touched upon the three pivotal principles that have been the compass of my life's journey. We looked at understanding our audience and ourselves, but there are two more principles to explore: What Am I Doing Here? and What Was I Thinking?

What Am I Doing Here?

It's not merely about the physical space we occupy, but also the company we keep. Our associations and the communities we immerse ourselves in speak volumes about our character, desires, and fears. This upcoming work will help us analyze our surroundings, learn from our choices, and understand how our associations can transform us.

What Was I Thinking?

Decision-making is an art, one that we rarely give its due importance. From impulsive choices to those pondered over sleepless nights, every decision carves a chapter in the story of our lives. This book will explore decision-making, including its brilliance and pitfalls. It's a journey to celebrate the beauty of good choices and to learn gracefully from the bad ones.

Stay tuned. These interesting continuations of our exploration into self-awareness and human interaction are under development.

Made in the USA
Monee, IL
26 December 2024